SPOTLIGHT
ON CHILDREN'S
AUTHORS

# CORNELIA FUNKE

SUE CORBETT

Cavendish
Square

New York

Published in 2014 by Cavendish Square Publishing, LLC
303 Park Avenue South, Suite 1247, New York, NY 10010

Copyright © 2014 by Cavendish Square Publishing, LLC

First Edition

Library of Congress Cataloging-in-Publication Data

Corbett, Sue.
Cornelia Funke / Sue Corbett.
p. cm. — (Spotlight on children's authors)
Includes bibliographical references and index.
Summary: "Presents the biography of children's book author Cornelia Funke while exploring
her creative process as a writer and illustrator and the cultural impact of her work"—Provided by publisher.
ISBN 978-1-60870-930-4 (hardcover) — ISBN 978-1-62712-138-5 (paperback) — ISBN 978-1-60870-937-3 (ebook)
1. Funke, Cornelia Caroline—Juvenile literature. 2. Authors, German—20th century—Biography—Juvenile literature.
3. Illustrators—Germany—Biography—Juvenile literature. 4. Children's literature, German—Authorship—
Juvenile literature. I. Title.
PT2666.U49Z56 2013
833'.914—dc23
[B]
2012007851

Senior Editor: Deborah Grahame-Smith
Art Director: Anahid Hamparian
Series Designer: Kay Petronio

Photo research by Lindsay Aveilhe
Cover photo courtesy of Marcus Brandt/dpa/picture-alliance/Newscom

The photographs in this book with permission and through courtesy of:
Florian Jaenicke/laif/Redux: p. 4; Bastian Parschau/Getty Images: p. 6; Werner Otto/Alamy: p. 9; Imagno/Getty Images: p. 10; Urbanmyth/Alamy: p. 12; Eisermann/laif/Redux: p. 15; Copyright © 2004 by Cornelia Funke. Published by Chicken House, an imprint of Scholastic, Inc.: p. 18; AF archive/Alamy: p. 21; Copyright © 2010 by Cornelia Funke. Published by Scholastic, Inc.: p. 24; DR2 WENN Photos/Newscom: p. 30; Foto Pollex/Action Press /ZUMA Press/Newscom: p. 33; Fuhr/Agency People Image/FUHR/SIPA/Newscom: p. 36

Printed in the United States of America

# CONTENTS

INTRODUCTION: A Letter to the Editor (Who Published Harry Potter)

In 2001, a ten-year-old English schoolgirl named Clara George received a book as a Christmas gift from her cousins, who lived in Germany. The title of the book was *Herr der Diebe,* and it was written in German, her mother's native language. "I couldn't read German myself yet," Clara remembered, so her mother read it aloud to her.

Clara loved the book. She wanted to read it again, by herself, and recommend it to her friends. She wondered why such a terrific book had not been translated into English.

At the same time, in Hamburg, Germany, the author of *Herr der Diebe* was wondering pretty much the same thing. She had asked her cousin to translate the book into English and had sent copies to various publishers in England. No one had expressed an interest.

Clara did not know the author of *Herr der Diebe*—yet. But her aunt, Elinor, worked for a British publisher. Clara told her aunt that kids like her, who loved the

Harry Potter series, would also love *Herr der Diebe*. Aunt Elinor suggested that Clara write to the man who had published J. K. Rowling's books in England and tell him about *Herr der Diebe*. Clara addressed her letter to "The Editor Who Published Harry Potter."

That editor's name was Barry Cunningham. "Normally we do not seek out books that are recommended to us by people who send in letters," he recalled. "But it was lovely that this recommendation was coming from a child, and Clara had very cleverly listed the ingredients that she thought made the book so successful—a gang of runaway children, a grumpy detective, a magical carousel. It sounded like a recipe for a great adventure, so we made it our business straightaway to find this book that had so enchanted this little girl."

Cunningham did find the book, and he did publish it in English. The translated title was *The Thief Lord*. And the author was Cornelia Funke, who went on to work with Cunningham to bring many of her other books—*Dragon Rider*, *Inkheart*, and *Igraine the Brave*—to English-language audiences.

And it turned out Clara was right. Very right. Her schoolmates—and millions of other English-speaking kids—did love *The Thief Lord*.

The area where Cornelia grew up is home
to many "water castles," huge fortress-style buildings,
many of which are surrounded by moats.

# Chapter 1
# A (FAIRY) GODMOTHER

**Karl and Wilhelmina Funke** intended to name their firstborn child after a favorite relative, but when the relative found out, she put an end to that plan.

"She saved me from being Hildegunde," Cornelia said of her aunt. "She told my parents, 'If you name her that, I will *not* be the godmother.'"

Instead, the baby girl, born in 1958, was christened Cornelia, an Italian name that planted a fondness for Italy in the future writer's heart from a very early age. (Aunt Hildegunde happily became her godmother.) Two years later, a brother, Volker, joined the family. He was followed by a second boy, Elmar, and finally, fourteen years after Cornelia's birth, a sister, Insa.

The family lived on the outskirts of Dorsten, the northernmost town in an industrial and highly populated part of Germany. Dorsten is closer to Germany's border with the Netherlands than it is to the German city of Frankfurt. London, England, is due west, about 360 miles (580 kilometers) away.

Americans think of places like Boston and Philadelphia as cities drenched in history. Here is a bit of perspective: Archaeological findings show that Dorsten had residents as early as 4000 BCE. The Romans had a military post there in the eleventh century BCE. The area became known as Dorsten nearly four centuries *before* the first European settler arrived in Boston or Philadelphia!

Growing up in an ancient region of the world has its advantages for a writer of fantasies. The rural area just north of Dorsten not only has a great name—Münsterland—but also is home to hundreds of castles ringed by moats, just like the ones you might read about in a fairy tale. "There was a girl in my class at school who actually was a baroness," Cornelia remembered.

Dorsten itself, however, was a working-class town, still rebuilding after it had been nearly destroyed in British bombing raids during World War II. "They rebuilt, but it was from the ruins, literally picking the stones from the rubble to rebuild the church and the mayor's house and then paint over it," Cornelia remembered. "My grandfather showed me photographs of Dorsten from before the war, and they did not resemble the town I knew at all."

Cornelia spent her early years on the outskirts of town. "[I had] a very clichéd childhood," she said. "Children in the streets all day until your mother called you home. We were filthy by then, from playing in the canals, or in the fields." She admits to being a "bossy big sister" to Volker and Elmar. She would invent new story lines for their favorite television series—*Star Trek*—to keep them entertained.

By the time Cornelia was a teenager, her family had moved to the center of town, where her father was a clerk at the courthouse. She did not like central Dorsten nearly as much as the countryside, but in a way this new environment set up her future. The teenage Cornelia became a "bit of a bookworm. That little town felt so small and ugly. Books were my windows and doors to other places, better places, bigger places."

Cornelia's hometown, Dorsten, was destroyed by bombs during World War II and rebuilt from salvaged rubble afterward.

As a student, Cornelia admitted, she could be lazy when the topic did not interest her, but she demonstrated a passion for words. Her favorite subjects were German and English literature. "I loved to write essays, though always too long and not always strict on the topic," she said.

Despite Cornelia's love of essays, however, she did not envision a career as a writer. "I wanted to be an astronaut, later on, a pilot, or live with the 'Red Indians,'" she writes on her website. She traces her fascination with Native Americans to a series by German author Karl May, who wrote more than seventy novels, set in the American Wild West, without ever having traveled to the United States. "It was all made up," Cornelia said. "But I was hugely impressed. When I was a teen, I was determined I would marry a Native American chief."

Like these two German children (shown welcoming Osage chieftain White Horse Eagle to Berlin in the 1930s), Cornelia became fascinated with Native Americans after reading the novels of author Karl May.

Cornelia's godmother, Hildegunde Latsch, reinforced her niece's interest in stories. A teacher of German, Hildegunde lived in Africa for much of the time Cornelia was growing up, but she always gave Cornelia books as gifts. "She introduced me to the German poets and the German dramatists," Cornelia remembered.

Cornelia also showed skill at drawing. Another relative—an uncle who was an art professor—encouraged her to refine her talents by enrolling in art school after high school. Cornelia resisted. "What [could] I do with that?" she wondered. "It was too impractical."

By the time Cornelia was finishing high school and was faced with making decisions about her future, she was sure of one thing: she wanted to work with children. Her sister, Insa, was four years old when Cornelia was eighteen. "I was completely enchanted with her," Cornelia remembered. But the school counselor said Cornelia would need more education. The counselor said, "You can't just go work in the kindergarten. You have to go to college and study education."

Cornelia was not sure if she wanted to be a teacher, but she *was* anxious to leave Dorsten and to see the wider world. Another development made up her mind: Aunt Hildegunde had returned from Africa and had settled in Hamburg, only a few hours north of Dorsten. Hildegunde invited Cornelia to live with her family, which now included two young sons, while Cornelia attended classes at the University of Hamburg.

At age eighteen, Cornelia left Dorsten for the big city.

## IT'S NOT FUNKY

*Funke* is a common German word that means "spark." Many native English speakers have trouble pronouncing it. The correct pronunciation is FOON-kah. But, Cornelia says, "a lot of people say 'Funky,' and I rather like that."

Hamburg, built on the banks of the Elbe River,
is the second-largest city in Germany and home
to one of the busiest ports in Europe.

# Chapter 2
# LIVING AGAINST YOUR GIFTS

Hamburg is a port city with nearly 2 million residents. (By comparison, Dorsten's population is about 80,000.) When Cornelia arrived in 1976, Hamburg was a thriving metropolis and the second-largest city in Germany. She took her school counselor's advice and majored in education at the university.

Living with Aunt Hildegunde meant getting to spend more time with Cornelia's young cousins, Oliver, then seven, and Wolfram, age ten. "I was like a big sister to them," she said.

School, however, was not as much fun. Cornelia found the education courses incredibly dull. "There were a lot of really boring lessons, all about theory, when I was hungry for practical work." But she got through it, and after graduating, Cornelia took two big steps toward finding more satisfying work. She enrolled in a course in book illustration at the Hamburg State College of Design—"as a treat to myself," she said— and found a job where she could work with children without having to be a schoolteacher.

"When I finished school I wanted to change the world, and I thought the best way would be to become a social worker," Cornelia said. She calls the place where she worked an "adventure playground," but in the United States, a closer equivalent would be something like the Boys and Girls Club. It was a center where children could play, learn, and feel safe during the hours they were not in school.

The center where Cornelia worked was open to children between the ages of three and eighteen. The kids did not have to register or even give their names, because such requirements might mean some children would not come at all. "These were children who might never be able to get a signature from a parent," Cornelia said.

There was no fee, and children could come and go as they pleased. "One day we would have ten children come in; the next day, fifty," recalled Cornelia. The facility was in a guarded area and had a playground, arts and crafts tables, and a big selection of books.

"These were children whose fathers were in prison or, perhaps, who had no parents at all," Cornelia remembered. The staff taught them practical skills—how to build a fire or plant potatoes—or guided the children in play. "We would paint with them or read to them—give them skills that made them feel good about themselves," said Cornelia.

Cornelia loved the children and felt utterly changed by them. "Many of them came from very difficult backgrounds and dysfunctional families, but I respected them so much for their courage and their compassion for one another," she said. "I saw them care for their siblings, where their parents didn't care at all. I saw them laugh, although life didn't give them much to laugh about."

After three years at the center, Cornelia decided to do something different. In 1981 she had fallen in love and married Rolf Frahm, a printer and bookbinder she met while still a university student. Cornelia's job was taking an emotional toll on her: "I could not change the world of

Cornelia married Rolf
Frahm, a printer and
bookbinder, in 1981.

these children, as much as I wanted to. It was a very hard decision to
leave because I felt I was betraying them."

Cornelia realized that when she was at the center, she spent most of
her time reading aloud to the children or helping with their art projects.
Books and pictures: These were the things Cornelia had been drawn to
all her life. With her art school training completed, she decided to seek
work as an illustrator. "I had wanted to make the world a better place,
but I found out, you can't live against your gifts. And my gifts are writing
and drawing," she said.

At first, Cornelia found work designing board games and illustrating
books for other authors. Her first jobs required oodles of work for very
little pay. But each time she got an assignment, she and Rolf would

celebrate with a little chocolate cake from their favorite bakery. Within a few years, she became a sought-after illustrator. She knew she was on her way to a successful career when she and Rolf decided she had too many jobs to have chocolate cake every time she got a new one.

Cornelia worked for several years to establish herself as an illustrator before taking on the next challenge. "I was, I have to admit, bored by the stories I had to illustrate," she explained. The manuscripts were typically about realistic events—familiar situations at school or at home. But Cornelia had noticed that the stories most likely to capture the attention of the children at the center had been the exciting and magical ones—fantastic adventures that took them away from the world they knew. As an artist, Cornelia was also looking for subjects that would be interesting to illustrate. She wanted to draw fairies and ogres, griffins and dragons, and put them in enchanted settings, like the moated castles back home in Münsterland.

One night, when Cornelia was twenty-eight years old, she started to write her own book, titled *The Dragon Quest*. Unlike most first-time writers, Cornelia did not have any trouble finding a publisher who wanted to buy it. She sent the manuscript to four German publishers. One said, "No, thanks." The other three said yes! She took the best offer.

Coming up with ideas has never been a problem for Cornelia. After the publication of *The Dragon Quest*, she quickly went on to produce many other books, most of which she illustrated herself. These books were short and aimed at readers in early elementary school. Cornelia became a star in Germany. She was the author of two of the nation's most popular series of short chapter books for new readers: *Ghosthunters* and *The Wild Chicks*. (*Ghosthunters* has since been published in the United

States, and two of five of *The Wild Chicks* books, renamed *C.H.I.X.* in the English translation, have been published in the United Kingtom.)

While Cornelia was producing all these books, she and Rolf became parents. Their first child, Anna, was born in 1989. In 1994, their second child, Ben, was born. The family lived on the outskirts of Hamburg, in the countryside, where the children could spend a lot of time outdoors as Cornelia had when she was a girl in Dorsten. The Funkes even had their own horses.

By the mid-1990s, Cornelia had written and illustrated dozens of books, and she had two children to keep her busy when she was away from her writing desk. Life was good. And she might still be living in Hamburg, unknown to the non-German-speaking world, if it weren't for a TV producer who read her very first book, *The Dragon Quest,* and liked it very much—so much that he asked to see more.

## FROM FRAHM TO FUNKE

Cornelia used her original surname, Funke, when she was first published. Rolf's last name was Frahm. But when Anna was about four, she marched up to her parents and announced that she wanted to be a Funke, too. According to Cornelia, Rolf responded, "I never liked the name Frahm myself." So the whole family adopted Cornelia's surname.

Cornelia's first full-fledged novel was published in Germany (titled *Drachenreiter*) in 1997. Years later, it was translated into English and published in America as *Dragon Rider*.

# Chapter 3
# A DRAGON, A REVELATION, AND A THIEF

A German television producer wanted to turn Cornelia's first book, *The Dragon Quest*, into a cartoon show. But the book was very short, so he asked Cornelia if she could "stretch" the text.

"You can't just stretch a story," she explained to him. She was also concerned that just adding ideas to the original story would make it boring.

Instead, Cornelia decided to write a new dragon adventure. "For the first time, I planned a really long book," she said. She had always wanted to ride a dragon herself, so she started with that idea. She created a young, silver-scaled dragon named Firedrake and gave him a quest: to find the mythical Rim of Heaven in the Himalayas and to see if it will work as a new home for his clan, whose current valley is about to be overrun by humans. Firedrake is joined on his journey by Sorrel, a wisecracking brownie (a type of fairy), as well as a human boy named Ben—which is also the name of Cornelia's son, who was a toddler when she was writing the book.

It took Cornelia more than a year to finish the book, and when she did, she liked what she had written so much that she decided she didn't want it to be a cartoon show after all. *Dragon Rider* (the German title is *Drachenreiter*) was published in 1997. Most German children were not intimidated by its length—more than five hundred pages.

The real significance of *Dragon Rider* for Cornelia was not that it became a best seller or was published in several languages—even though both happened. The real importance of *Dragon Rider* was that it made Cornelia realize that her real calling was not illustration; it was storytelling. While artwork had given her a way into the world of book publishing, it was writing stories that gave her the most satisfaction. She couldn't wait to dig in to another one, and she already knew where she would set it: Venice, Italy.

Cornelia had been to Venice many times as a tourist. She, Rolf, and Anna once had rented a cottage there for three months. (If you are from a mostly chilly place like northwestern Germany, the warm Italian sun is quite a magnet.) "It's the perfect place for children, because there are no cars," Cornelia said. The many alleyways and canals of Venice seemed like an ideal location for an adventure full of intrigue, as there are hundreds of places to hide.

An avid reader of fantasies, Cornelia also liked that Venice was a real place. "I wanted to tell children that there is a place in this world that is real and full of history, but also contains magic and mystery," she explained. "You can't actually get to Hogwarts or Narnia, but you can get to Venice."

Indeed, Venice had bewitched her, just as it had bewitched Bo and Prosper's mother in what would become Cornelia's next book. This was the novel that would make her famous not just in Germany but around the world: *The Thief Lord*.

At the center of *The Thief Lord*'s story are two orphans, twelve-year-old Prosper and his five-year-old brother, Bo, who run away from Hamburg to Venice because their aunt and uncle want to keep Bo but send Prosper to boarding school. The boys can't bear the thought of being separated.

When they arrive in Venice, they fall in with a band of orphans led by Scipio, a boy who wears a mask and calls himself the Thief Lord. Scipio finds the gang a hideout in an abandoned movie theater and brings them stolen loot to fence (sell to others). The children are just getting by, with Venice's cold winter descending, when they discover they are being tracked by a detective, hired by Prosper and Bo's aunt and uncle.

The story does have a magical element—a long-lost carousel that reportedly has the power to "make adults out of children and children out of adults"—but the characters come straight from Cornelia's memories of the real children she cared for at the "adventure playground" in Hamburg. "I tried to create children who cared for each other even under the worst circumstances, even if they are left alone by their parents," Cornelia said.

When the book was released in Germany in 2000, it became a phenomenal success.

That same year, just a few hundred miles west of Hamburg, another writer's books were setting the wider world on fire. J. K. Rowling, the

Cornelia poses with the cast of *The Thief Lord*, her second novel, which was made into a film in 2006.

creator of Harry Potter, had already published the first three books in her series about the boy wizard and was quickly becoming not only one of the most famous writers on Earth but also—and more significantly to Cornelia—one of the most widely read authors in the school yard. Rowling's publisher planned to print one million copies of her fourth book, *Harry Potter and the Goblet of Fire.*

Cornelia believed that children who liked Harry Potter would also like *Dragon Rider* and *The Thief Lord,* if only she could get someone to publish them in English. She asked her cousin Oliver Latsch, who is a literary agent today, to translate her books into English. Because Oliver had spent part of his childhood in Zimbabwe, a former British colony that includes English as one of its three official languages, his English was very good.

Cornelia's translated manuscripts made the rounds of the top British publishers. Several companies showed an interest, but nobody had actually made an offer by the time young Clara George's letter, addressed to "The Editor Who Published Harry Potter," reached the desk of Barry Cunningham.

After acquiring the Harry Potter series for another publisher, Cunningham had struck out on his own and founded Chicken House Publishing in 2000. Cunningham already had a long career in publishing and a reputation for taking chances on new writers. (Much to their regret, more than a dozen other publishers had rejected the first Harry Potter book before Cunningham bought the manuscript for an advance of about $2,500.)

Cunningham tracked down Funke's agent in Hamburg, read her manuscripts, and immediately bought the English-language rights for *Herr der Diebe* and *Drachenreiter.* Cunningham thought *The Thief*

*Lord* would make a stronger first impression in the English-speaking world, so he decided to publish it first, even though Cornelia had written it second.

In July 2000, *The Thief Lord* went on sale in England. The first printing sold out in just ten days, an unheard-of phenomenon for a children's book. Scholastic, which publishes Chicken House books in the United States, was now interested as well. Would Cunningham produce a version for American readers?

"Books in translation are often good deeds but not good sellers," Cunningham explained. Books that are best sellers in their own countries sometimes do not resonate with audiences in other places. However, publishers have long believed that sharing stories across borders is an easy way to build bridges between countries and cultures.

After an editor or a publisher, like Cunningham, acquires a manuscript, he or she must first sell it to the company's sales representatives. Sales representatives are the publishing employees whose job it is to convince bookstore owners and librarians that a particular book is worth stocking on their shelves. For a book to do really well, the sales reps have to be excited about it.

Cunningham was a bit worried about presenting *The Thief Lord* to Scholastic's sales reps. "I remember standing at the sales conference being terribly enthusiastic about this new book, translated from the German, set in Venice, with a glossary of Italian words at the back, and, oh, yes, it is more than 500 pages long," he said. "To their credit, the Scholastic people assured me, 'Well, Barry, if you say it's a good book, we believe you.'"

Later they were very glad they had trusted his judgment.

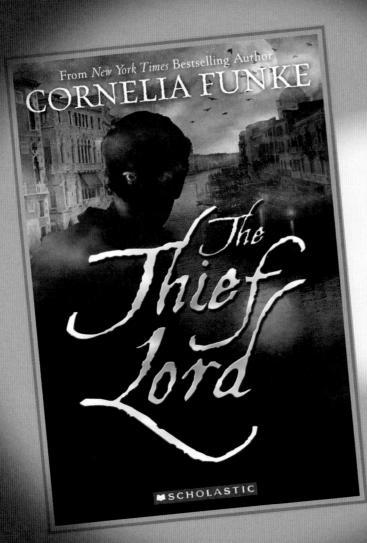

From *New York Times* Bestselling Author

# CORNELIA FUNKE

## The Thief Lord

**SCHOLASTIC**

Cornelia's life changed forever with the English-language translation of *The Thief Lord.*

# Chapter 4
## INKY VILLAINS

*The Thief Lord* made Cornelia an international star. Critics called the book an immediate classic, and it spent more than six months on the *New York Times* best-seller list. *School Library Journal* and *Parenting* magazine both named it one of their best books of the year. It also won a slew of awards, including the prestigious Mildred L. Batchelder Award, which is presented annually by the American Library Association to the most outstanding book originally published in a language other than English and then translated and published in the United States.

Sometimes books in translation are good deeds *and* best sellers. *The Thief Lord* has since been published in nearly fifty languages.

To promote the book in the United States, Scholastic brought Cornelia to America twice in 2002—first, to meet booksellers before the book was published, and second, for a fall tour to New York, San Francisco, Denver, and Chicago. Cornelia was excited but nervous about these trips. She had to leave her children, Anna and Ben, then ages thirteen and eight, in Hamburg. She spoke English, but not perfectly. Her publicists at Scholastic were setting up interviews with television and newspaper reporters, and she had been invited to appear at bookstores across the country.

"She was reluctant to come mostly because it was a problem for her to be away from her family," Barry Cunningham remembered. "And she was very, very worried about her English. But she looks every inch the fairy storyteller from Europe with her blond hair and her big passion for stories, and that more than compensated for the not-quite-perfect English."

Indeed, the trip had an outcome that Cornelia never foresaw: she fell in love with America. The children she met on tour asked interesting questions and were genuinely curious about her books. Cornelia was surprised that so many of the people she met were as passionate about books and reading as she was. "I was especially enchanted by the book maniacs in America. I didn't know there [were] so many here," she said. "I have to confess this kind of book passion I have only [found] in America."

While *The Thief Lord* was winning Cornelia fans across the globe, she returned to Hamburg eager to finish her work in progress: *Inkheart*.

The story idea for *Inkheart* began with an image Cornelia could not get out of her head: "A girl sitting in her bed while outside the house a figure is standing in the rain," she remembered. The figure outside is the character of Dustfinger, who arrived almost fully formed in Cornelia's imagination: "He told me his name, and he was so real that after a while I had the feeling that he was standing behind me whispering his story in my ear."

Again, Cornelia set the novel in her heart's place: Italy. She had always wanted to write a story in which the characters come to life. In *Inkheart*, Mo Folchart, the father of twelve-year-old Meggie, reads aloud so well that the characters from the book he is reading (itself titled

*Inkheart,* written by a fictional author named Fenoglio) step out of the story and into the real world. At the same moment, however, Meggie's beloved mother, Resa, and two cats trade places with Dustfinger and two villains. Dustfinger and the villains come out of the book, and Resa and the cats become trapped inside it. One of the villains, named Capricorn, is described as so evil that he would "feed a bird to a cat on purpose, just to watch it being torn apart." Mo has hidden from Capricorn for years, because he knows that the villain would like to use Mo's magical talent for his own purposes. Finally, Capricorn realizes that the way to get Mo to do his bidding is to kidnap Meggie and use her as bait.

## AN INSPIRING ACTOR

Cornelia has said that she signed on with publisher Barry Cunningham because he reminded her of one of her favorite actors, Bob Hoskins. She also chose an actor—Brendan Fraser—as her model for Mo Folchart, in part because her children had enjoyed his performance in *George of the Jungle.* She sent him one of the first copies of *Inkheart,* personally inscribed with a thank-you for inspiring the character. Fraser was so flattered that he and Funke became friends, and when it came time to make the movie based on *Inkheart,* Cornelia insisted he play the role.

Released in October 2003, *Inkheart* quickly made the *New York Times* best-seller list, where it remained for months. *Publishers Weekly* called the book "delectably transfixing," and in *Time* magazine, author Clive

## FENOGLIO AND FIREDRAKE

Cornelia has had many requests from readers to write the book about Dustfinger and Capricorn that the character Mo reads aloud within *Inkheart*. She laughed when recalling what her publisher, Barry Cunningham, told one person who made that suggestion: "He said, 'She can't possibly write that! Fenoglio writes in a completely different style than Cornelia.'"

A young reader once asked Cornelia, "If you had Mo's ability to read a character out of a book, who would you choose?" Without hesitation, Cornelia said she would bring Firedrake to life—so she could get her own ride on a dragon.

Barker said *Inkheart* was Cornelia's "most elegant and accomplished work to date." Cornelia's publisher, Barry Cunningham, believes that the book's wide appeal stemmed from every reader's secret desire to be a character in a favorite book. "It was a good idea that she developed in a very interesting way," he said. "What happens if you are caught in the story because, now that you're in the book, the story changes? How do you deal with that?"

Although *Inkheart* derives considerable tension from the actions of its villains, it is more than an adventure story; it is also a valentine to books and readers. Meggie loves stories so much that she sleeps with whatever book she's reading under her pillow. When she and Mo must flee from place to place, the first things she packs are books for the journey. Cornelia has described herself as a passionate reader, and one of her goals as an author is to "try to awaken the passion for reading in children and adults." She works toward this goal in *Inkheart* by starting each chapter with a quotation from one of her favorite stories, which include *The Wind in the Willows,* the Lord of the Rings series, *Peter Pan,* and *Oliver Twist.* The books from which the quotations are taken constitute some of the most highly regarded literature ever written. It is as if Cornelia tucked a guide to great books into the pages of *Inkheart.*

"There are those people who love books and are greedy for books and the rustling of paper and the printed letter and I wanted to write about this," Cornelia said. "This lust for the printed word. And I think *Inkheart* is all about that. The enchantment that comes from books."

Hollywood came calling after Cornelia's books became best sellers. In fact, Cornelia wound up making Los Angeles her home address!

# Chapter 5
# COMING TO AMERICA

Following the success of *The Thief Lord* and *Inkheart*, Cornelia found herself very much in demand. American bookstore owners and readers wanted to meet the writer people were calling the German J. K. Rowling.

The biggest surprise to Cornelia was that she had also become much more famous at home. She credits this fame to the publication of a profile that appeared in the well-respected American newspaper the *Wall Street Journal*. In the article, writer Jeffrey A. Trachtenberg draws several parallels between *The Thief Lord* and the Harry Potter series and suggests that Cornelia's book could become the next huge hit imported from Europe. Immediately after the story appeared, "the German media exploded," Cornelia said. "Normally, they are not so interested in children's books, but this caused quite a stir."

TV and movie producers began calling Cornelia's publishers. The movie rights to *Inkheart* were sold to New Line Cinema, a Hollywood production company. German filmmakers were interested in making movie versions of Cornelia's books that had not yet been published in English—*The Wild Chicks* and *Hands Off Mississippi*. Scholastic planned an even longer U.S. tour to promote *Inkheart*, and it set off another wave of stories about Cornelia and her books.

## WRITE IT DOWN!

Cornelia never goes anywhere without a notebook, because ideas often come to her when she is traveling. (She once worked out a key scene involving Dustfinger while riding the subway in Hamburg.) She advises aspiring writers to record ideas immediately, so they aren't forgotten. Always carry something to write on, Cornelia said, "or at least have a pen that writes on skin."

By this point, Cornelia was well into writing *Inkspell*, the second book in her Inkworld trilogy. (She hadn't known she was writing a trilogy when she had started *Inkheart*, but "the story wouldn't leave me alone," she said.) With two school-age children, deadlines for publishers in three countries, and pitches from television and film producers to consider, she had a lot on her plate. Cornelia would have liked to just disappear into Inkworld and finish her story, but her popularity was still gaining momentum. The American Booksellers Association gave *Inkheart* one of its most prestigious awards. Scholastic decided to publish several of her picture books, including *The Princess Knight* and *Pirate Girl*. And Cornelia had to make decisions about various aspects of the *Inkheart* film. The bookish girl from Dorsten was suddenly at the center of a storm of activity.

It's not like Cornelia was an overnight sensation. By this time, she had been illustrating and writing children's books for nearly two decades. Before Cornelia had published even one copy of a book in English, she had written more than forty in her native country and had total sales of more than a million copies. No one in Germany had ever made such a fuss over her.

## I AM IGRAINE

Cornelia says there is a bit of herself in almost all of her characters, but the one who resembles her most closely is Igraine the Brave.

But her audience had changed—it had become much, much larger. And most of it was not in Hamburg; it was west across the North Sea in the United Kingdom, and west again across the Atlantic Ocean. Could Cornelia manage all the demands on her time and still live on the outskirts of Hamburg? Did she *want* to?

"Children's authors in Germany were not given the kind of imaginative respect they are given in England and America," said Cornelia's publisher, Barry Cunningham. "American culture was more open to welcoming her as a storyteller in all its guises."

Cornelia and Rolf made a big decision: the whole Funke family would move to Los Angeles, California, where the sun would warm them. Cornelia would be closer to the people who wanted to make movies out of her books. And Anna and Ben would have the experience of living in another country.

The books Cornelia loves to autograph are the ones that are a little beat up or careworn — evidence that they have been read!

## AN ARTIST AT HEART

Perhaps because of her background in illustration, Cornelia still envisions her books on storyboards before she begins writing them. The walls of her writing cottage are covered with her drawings.

The Funkes arrived in Beverly Hills in 2005 and bought a house that sits on a lushly landscaped piece of property at the base of a canyon. (Actress Faye Dunaway once owned the house.) A small building in the backyard became Cornelia's writing cottage. It has bookshelves lining the walls, a huge stained-glass window to let in spangled light, and a big desk.

Cornelia felt immediately that they made the right decision. "I have never felt so much at home in a place," she said.

Life was good. *Inkspell* was released in April 2005, the same month *Time* magazine listed Cornelia as one of the 100 most influential people in the world. Anna and Ben were flourishing in their new schools.

In her writing cottage, Cornelia began to work in earnest on the last book in the Inkworld trilogy, which had a working title of *Inkdawn*. On the final page of *Inkspell,* Farid, one of the main characters, whispers to Meggie, "This story will have a happy ending. I swear!" Cornelia was determined to make good on Farid's promise.

Within a year, however, Cornelia's own happiness was very much at stake. In February 2006, Rolf was diagnosed with colorectal cancer. He died four weeks later in a Los Angeles hospital. He was fifty-six years old. Cornelia was heartbroken. It was very hard to think about continuing to write stories when she had become a widow so suddenly.

"Rolf loved America as much as Cornelia did," her publisher, Barry Cunningham, recalled. "His death was sad, and unexpected. And it made writing the last book [of the Inkworld trilogy] very painful because she had to deal with some dark issues."

By the time Cornelia finished it, *Inkdawn* had become *Inkdeath*. The book is dedicated to Rolf, her husband of twenty-five years, a man who had shared chocolate cakes with her when just getting an assignment was cause for celebration. The inscription reads:

> To Rolf, always—it was the best of things
> to be married to Dustfinger

Cornelia attends a 2008 event in Berlin
with her son, Ben, and daughter, Anna.

# Chapter 6
# WHAT'S NEXT FOR CORNELIA?

The loss of Rolf still weighs on Cornelia. She told an interviewer he was the only one who could get her illustrations to her publishers without bending them in the process.

Now that Anna has gone off to study art history in England, it's just Cornelia, Ben, and Luna, their big shaggy dog, in Los Angeles.

But Cornelia has many stories left to write. In fact, she is sure she will never find time to turn all of her ideas into books.

In 2010, she introduced the first book in a new series, *Reckless,* which she wrote with a collaborator named Lionel Wigram. Wigram is more famous in Hollywood than in literary circles, as he was the executive producer of all the Harry Potter movies. Cornelia and Lionel are planning two more books, and the second installment, *Fearless*, is scheduled for release in 2013.

Cornelia also has finished a stand-alone novel released in May 2012 called *Ghost Knight*. The original idea for this book came to her while she was sightseeing during a visit to her British publisher. "The moment I stepped into Salisbury Cathedral I knew I had come to one of those places soaked in stories and magic," Cornelia said. "The last time I had felt like that had been in Venice!" Cornelia wrote the story in first

## CHECK HER OUT!

If Cornelia were a book, she'd like to be a library book, "so I would be taken home by all different sorts of kids. A library book, I imagine, is a happy book."

person—the first time she had tried that approach in a novel.

Film and television producers continue to capitalize on Cornelia's work. Her delightful chapter book *When Santa Fell to Earth* was made into a movie in Germany in 2011. Cornelia is also working on adapting some of her stories for the stage.

Equally as important as Cornelia's writing is making sure she finds time to help children like those who first inspired her to write. Cornelia felt guilty when she left her job as a social worker, but she feels she's been able to do plenty for children by using her talents to their full extent. Today she is a donor to nearly a dozen charities that serve children.

"My talents have luckily brought me enough fame and money to support children all over the world: children who are sick, disfigured, or abused. Children who fled war and need a new home. Children who aren't loved or face death in a hospital," Cornelia said. "A wonderful doctor here in Los Angeles who has been working with abused children for many years said a very true thing to me: 'Cornelia, we both can face a sad story, but only if we can give it a better ending.'"

# CORNELIA LIKES TO READ:

Cornelia believes she has read enough books in her lifetime to fill an entire library, but each of them taught her something about writing and storytelling. There are a few (more than a dozen!) that she considers unforgettable. These are the books she reads over and over again.

*The BFG* by Roald Dahl

*The Brothers Lionheart* by Astrid Lindgren

The Chronicles of Narnia series by C. S. Lewis

*The Graveyard Book* by Neil Gaiman

*Jim Button* and *Luke the Engine Driver* by Michael Ende

*Just So Stories* by Rudyard Kipling

The Lord of the Rings series by J. R. R. Tolkien

*The Once and Future King* by T. H. White

*Peter Pan* by J. M. Barrie

*The Princess Bride* by William Goldman

*Skellig* by David Almond

*Tom Sawyer* by Mark Twain

*The War of the Buttons* by Louis Peraud

*Which Witch* by Eva Ibbotson

*The Wizard of Oz* by L. Frank Baum

# BOOKS BY CORNELIA FUNKE

(AVAILABLE IN ENGLISH)

## Novels

*The Thief Lord* (2002)

*Dragon Rider* (2004)

*When Santa Fell to Earth* (2006)

*Igraine the Brave* (2007)

*Reckless* (2010)

*Saving Mississippi* (2010)

*Ghost Knight* (2012)

## Ghosthunters Series

*Ghosthunters and the Incredibly Revolting Ghost* (2006)

*Ghosthunters and the Gruesome Invincible Lightning Ghost* (2006)

*Ghosthunters and the Totally Moldy Baroness!* (2007)

*Ghosthunters and the Muddy Monster of Doom!* (2007)

## The Inkworld Trilogy

*Inkheart* (2003)

*Inkspell* (2005)

*Inkdeath* (2008)

## C.H.I.X. Series

*The Summer Gang* (2012)

*The New Girl* (2012)

## Picture Books

*The Princess Knight* (2004), illustrated by Kerstin Meyer

*Pirate Girl* (2005), illustrated by Kerstin Meyer

*The Wildest Brother* (2006), illustrated by Kerstin Meyer

*Princess Pigsty* (2007), illustrated by Kerstin Meyer

# GLOSSARY

**baroness**—A noblewoman who belongs to the lowest rank of nobility.

**English-language rights**—The rights to produce an English-language version of a particular book, play, film, or other creative work that was not originally created in English.

**fence**—To buy or sell stolen goods.

**loot**—Stolen goods.

**resonate**—To produce a response in somebody, especially by reminding that person of something or prompting feelings of support or approval.

**revelation**—The exposure of something previously hidden or secret.

**work in progress**—An incomplete ongoing project, especially an artistic creation.

# CHRONOLOGY

**December 10, 1958:** Cornelia Caroline Funke is born in Dorsten, North Rhine, Westphalia, Germany.

**1980:** Cornelia graduates from the University of Hamburg with a degree in education theory.

**1981:** Cornelia marries Rolf Frahm.

**1989:** Their daughter, Anna, is born.

**1994:** Their son, Ben, is born.

**1997:** *Drachenreiter* (*Dragon Rider*) is published in Germany.

**2000:** *Herr der Diebe (The Thief Lord)* is published in Germany.

**2002:** *The Thief Lord* is published in the United States.

**2003:** *The Thief Lord* wins the Mildred L. Batchelder Award for the best translated children's book.

**2004:** *Inkheart* wins a Children's Literature Honor Book Award from the American Booksellers Association.

**2005:** *Time* magazine names Cornelia to its list of the world's 100 most influential people.

**May 2005:** Cornelia, Rolf, Anna, and Ben Funke move from Hamburg to Los Angeles, California.

**2006:** *Inkspell* wins the Children's Literature Book of the Year award from the American Booksellers Association.

**March 5, 2006:** Rolf Frahm Funke dies of cancer.

**2008:** *Inkdeath* is published.

**2010:** *Reckless* is published.

**2012:** *Ghost Knight* is published.

# FURTHER INFORMATION

## Books

Are you interested in trying to write stories yourself? These two books offer guidance:

Levine, Gail Carson. *Writing Magic*. New York: Collins, 2006.

Messner, Kate. *Real Revision: Authors' Strategies to Share with Student Writers*. Portland, ME: Stenhouse, 2011.

## Websites

Cornelia's website:

www.corneliafunke.com

Biographical information: www.scholastic.com/corneliafunke/bio.htm

Dedicated *Dragon Rider* site:
   www.scholastic.com/corneliafunke/dragonrider_rrr.asp

Dedicated *Inkheart* site: www.scholastic.com/inkheart/

*Inkheart* film website: www.au.warnerbros.com/inkheart/

Dedicated *Reckless* site: www.get-reckless.com/

# BIBLIOGRAPHY

## A note to report writers from Sue Corbett

To write this biography, I read Cornelia's books (well, the ones that have been published in English) and did research online. I read articles that had been written about Cornelia by other journalists. I had interviewed Cornelia myself several times, in my role as the children's book reviewer for the *Miami Herald*. I also spoke to people who had worked with Cornelia at three of her publishing houses.

Below is a list of sources I used. Any time *you* write a report, you should also keep track of where you got your information. It is fine to use information in your report if you found it somewhere else, as long as you give the source credit in a footnote, endnote, or note within the report itself. (Your teacher can tell you how he or she prefers you list your sources.)

It is not okay to pass off other people's work as your own.

### PRINT ARTICLES

Corbett, Sue. "Author on Her Way to Fame; Could Be Next J. K. Rowling." *Miami Herald*, December 2, 2003.

Maughan, Shannon. "Moving On Up: Fantasy, Film Tie-ins and Farts Sell Big to Kids." *Publishers Weekly*, November 14, 2002.

Review of *Inkheart. Publishers Weekly*, July 21, 2003, p. 196.

Review of *The Thief Lord. Publishers Weekly*, June 24, 2002, p. 57.

Sinkler, Rebecca Pepper. "Children's Books: Theft in Venice." *New York Times*, November 17, 2003.

Trachtenberg, Jeffrey A. "Pedigreed 'Harry' Wannabe—New Children's Book Parallels J. K. Rowling's in Many Ways; Author Is Success in Germany." *The Wall Street Journal*, July 15, 2002, p. B1ff.

Webb, James Neal. "Characters Come to Life in Fast-Paced Fantasy." *BookPage*, November 17, 2003.

## ONLINE SOURCES

"Cornelia Funke Biography." *Scholastic Books: The Stacks*. www.scholastic. com/titles/authors/Cornelia_funke.htm

"Cornelia Funke's Top 10 Bedtime Stories." *Guardian Unlimited*. www. guardian.co.uk/books/2003/oct/15/top10.bedtime.stories

*Inkheart* by Cornelia Funke (video interview). *Bookstream Inc./Bookwrap*. http://a1110.g.akamai.net/7/1110/5507/v002/bookstream.download.akamai. com/5507/bw/bs/0439531640/b1/default_wm.htm

"Talking with Cornelia Funke." *AudioFile*. www.audiofilemagazine.com/ features/A1222.html

# INDEX

# ABOUT THE AUTHOR:

Sue Corbett is a reporter who has worked for the *Miami Herald*, *People* magazine, and *Publishers Weekly*. She is also the author of several novels for kids, including *The Last Newspaper Boy in America*, *Free Baseball*, and *12 Again*.